GEOGRAPHY OF THE PLANETS! FAMOUS PLACES ON MARS, JUPITER, SATURN AND NEPTUNE SPACE FOR KIDS CHILDREN'S AERONAUTICS & SPACE BOOK

BABY PROFESSOR
EDUCATION KIDS

Planets are large objects
that orbit the Sun.

Mars, also known as the Red Planet, is the fourth planet from the Sun.

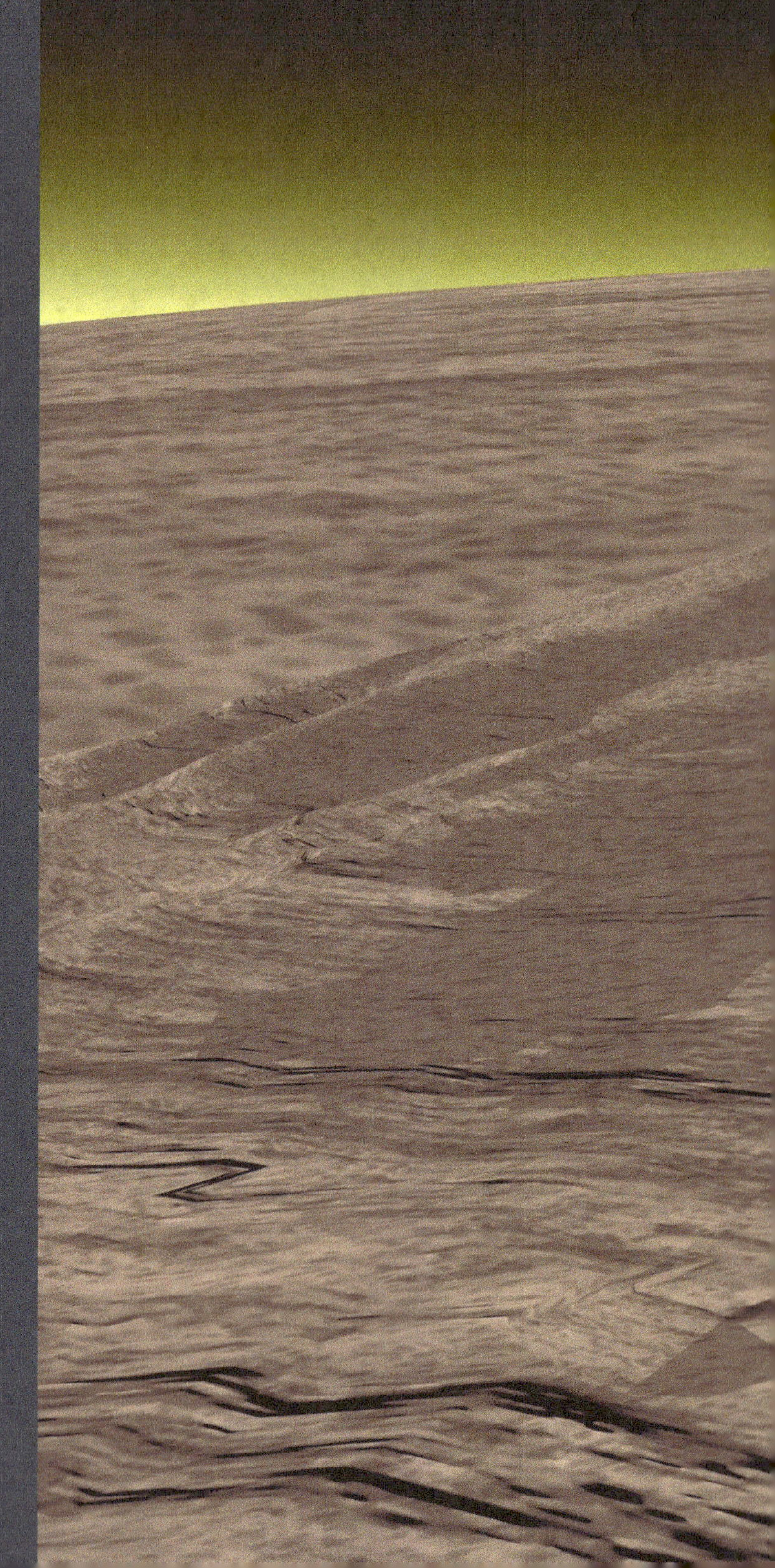

Olympus
Mons on
Mars is
the largest
volcano in
the Solar
System.

Valles Marineris is a big system of canyons on Mars. It's the longest in the Solar System.

Tharsis Bulge is a volcanic plateau on Mars. It is 23,000 feet above the surrounding plain.

The large
dark area
on Mars
is called
Cerberus.
Cerberus
Province
has about
nine
volcanoes.

Jupiter is
the fifth
planet from
the Sun.
It is the
stormiest
planet in
our solar
system.

TER

The Great Red Spot is a giant storm on Jupiter. Winds inside the storm reach up to 270 miles per hour.

Ganymede is the largest moon around Jupiter and in the solar system. The moon was discovered by Galileo Galilei.

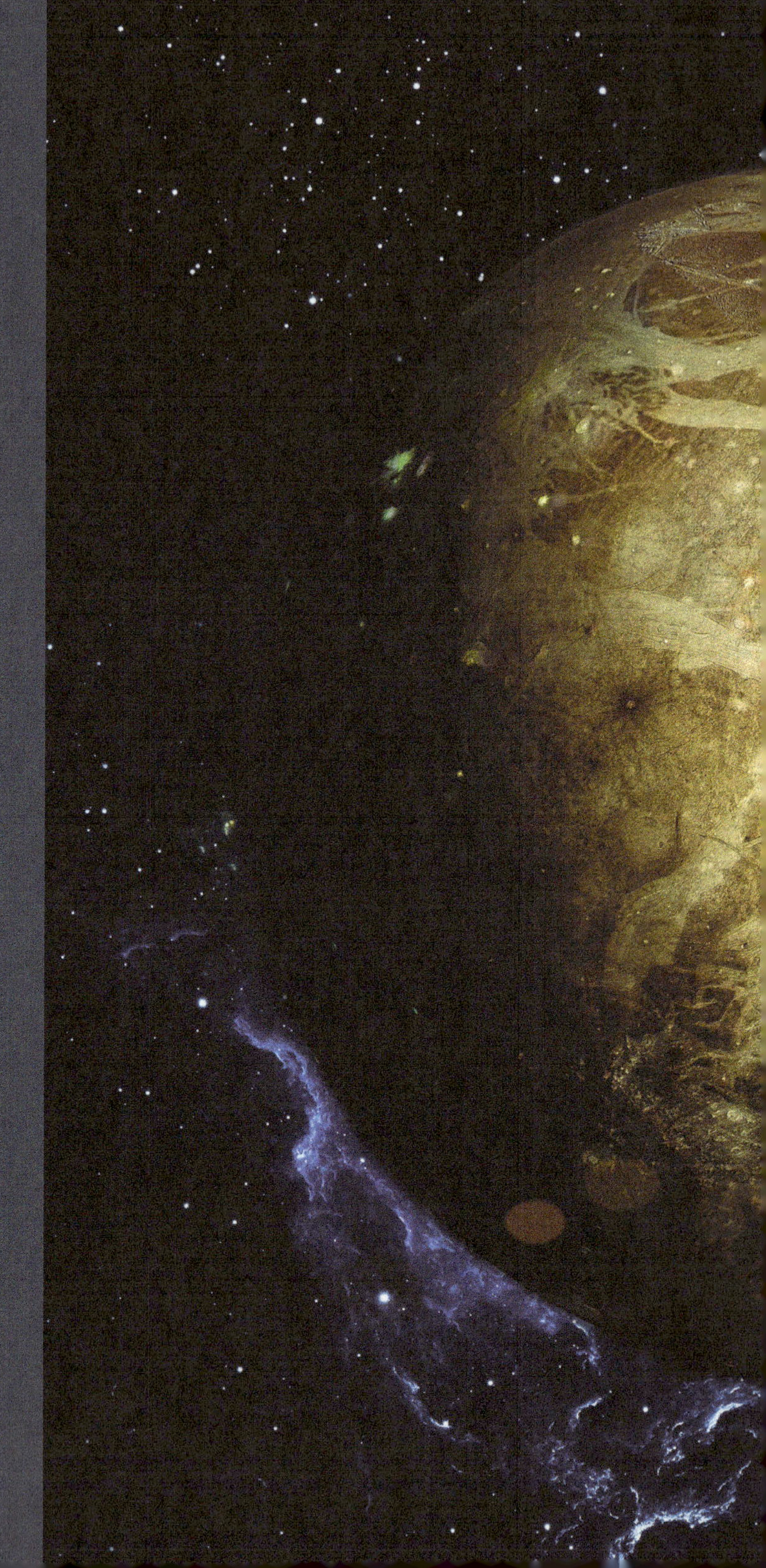

Io is one of Jupiter's moons. It has the most active volcanoes in the solar system.

Europa is
the sixth
moon of
Jupiter.
Scientists
believe that
a form of
life exists in
the oceans
of Europa.

Callisto is the second largest moon of Jupiter. It has the oldest landcape in the solar system.

Saturn is the
sixth planet
in our solar
system.
Saturn is
886 million
miles away
from
the sun.

Saturn is famous for its rings. Saturn's rings are made of up ice crystals.

Saturn's north pole has a hexagonal cloud pattern. It is a perfect six sided hurricane.

Titan is Saturn's largest moon. It is the only moon in our solar system that has clouds.

Neptune
is the 8th
planet from
the sun.
Neptune is
the windiest
planet in
our solar
system.

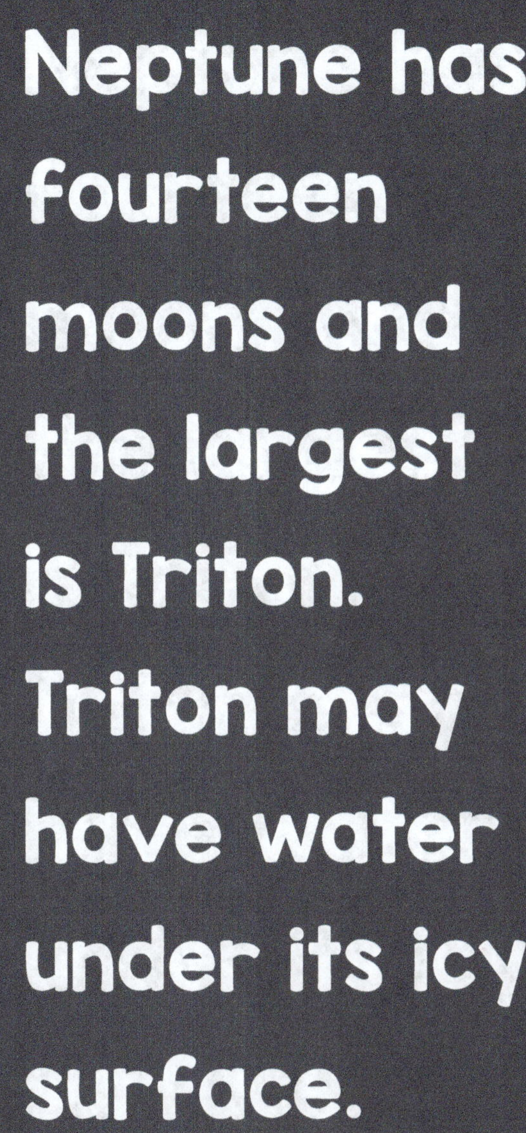

Neptune has fourteen moons and the largest is Triton. Triton may have water under its icy surface.

Did you
enjoy
reading
about the
planets?

Now it's
time for
you to share
this to your
friends.

Visit
BABY PROFESSOR
EDUCATION KIDS
www.BabyProfessorBooks.com
to download Free Baby Professor eBooks
and view our catalog of new and exciting
Children's Books